Crazy Graffiti

This splendid collection includes samples of wit from such varied sources as school classrooms and playgrounds, bus and railway stations, shops, libraries, canteens, swimming baths – even the farmyard. All are guaranteed to make you fall about with laughter!

Janet Rogers is the author of four more Beaver books which will keep you laughing: *The Crazy Joke Book*, *More Crazy Jokes*, *Even Crazier Jokes* and *The Craziest Joke Book Ever*.

CRAZY GRAFFITI!

JANET ROGERS

Illustrated By David Mostyn

Beaver Books

First published 1982 by
The Hamlyn Publishing Group Limited
London · New York · Sydney · Toronto
Astronaut House, Feltham, Middlesex, England

ISBN 0 600 20542 8

Printed and bound in Great Britain by
Cox & Wyman Limited, Reading

Contents

Introduction

GRaffiti rules, O.K.

I have been interested in graffiti for as long as I can remember, certainly ever since I scrawled my first words on the nursery wall. They were:

Infants Rool, O.K.

which I later discovered had been changed to:

Mother Rules, O.K.!

From the age of three onwards I have been fascinated by this original and exciting means of communication, and I am sure it was from walls not schools that I really learnt to read and write.

Believe it or not, graffiti has been around since long before you or even I was born. People say that in the Garden of Eden there was a particular apple tree that bore the message:

ADAM & EVE RULE, O.K.

and it's a fact that in a corner of Noah's Ark, scratched into the woodwork, could be seen:

Horses rule, Neigh, neigh

From the time when man first became able to communicate by writing, the graffiti craze has been spreading. In Britain graffiti has been known for hundreds of years. Take this typical Tudor example:

TOWN CRIERS rule, OYEZ! OYEZ! OYEZ!

.And today graffiti can be seen in the most unexpected places. Who, for example, was the elegant lady in a tiara seen spraying:

QUEEN ELIZABETH rules, U.K.

on the walls outside Buckingham Palace?

Schools, of course, present us with some very fine examples of the art and craft of graffiti. From the chemistry lab there is:

absolute Zero rules, 0°K°

from the mathematics department:

Slide Rules, $O^{x^2}\sqrt{K.^{sin}0.01^{x}}$

and from the staff room:

rules, RULE, O.K.

altered, of course, by public-spirited pupils to:

BREAK rules, OK!

Here, forming a historic and permanent record, are the very best of the scrawls of the walls preserved for all time in this major Beaver paperback. They come from schools, libraries, cinemas, the streets themselves – anywhere, in fact, where you might find a wall with writing on it. Some of them are my own originals, most of them are the work of my old friend Ann O'Nymous, and all of them are designed to entertain and educate you as no other form of literature can.

Remember, however, that graffiti should be seen to be read and never seen to be written, so if you want to write graffiti and you don't want to get into trouble write it on the facing page – *and nowhere else!*

HAVE FUN!

HAPPINESS IS A BLANK WHITE WALL

GRAFFITI IN THE CLASSROOM

JUST THINK: TOMORROW TODAY WILL BE YESTERDAY

RADIUM WAS DISCOVERED BY MADMAN CURRY

EGGHEADS OF THE WORLD UNITE! YOU HAVE NOTHING TO LOSE BUT YOUR YOKE

Yesterday I couldn't spell educated - NOW I ARE IT

THE WORLD IS FLAT
(SIGNED)-FORM IVb
1492

LOST: ONE SCIENCE TEACHER AFTER LAST WEDNESDAY'S EXPERIMENT

could you lose a french teacher next week?

I QUOTED THIS WALL IN MY EXAM AND PASSED

ISAAC NEWTON COUNTS ON HIS FINGERS

LATIN IS THE LANGUAGE OF THE DEAD

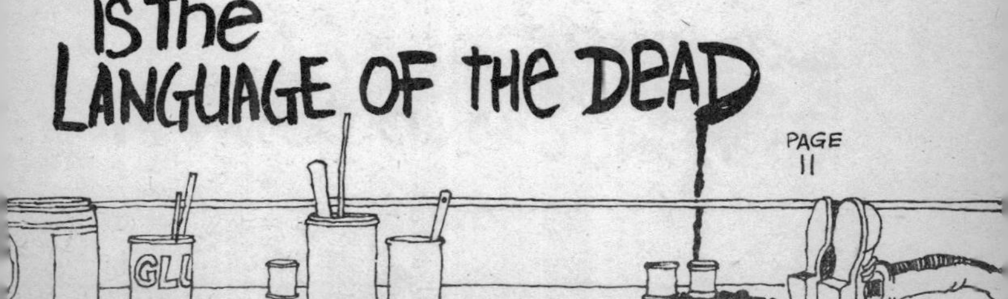

NOAH'S ARK WAS BIGGER THAN JOAN'S

YES, BUT JOAN'S WAS MAID OF ORLEANS

ARE LONDONERS DIM BECAUSE THE POPULATION'S SO DENSE?

CONFUCIUS HE SAY TOO MUCH

RICHARD COEUR DE LION-FIRST HEART TRANSPLANT

BOOTS, BOOTS,
BOOTS, BOOTS,
MARCHING UP AND DOWN ON SIR

I WANT TO LEAVE THE ROOM

WELL, YOU can't take it with you

DO VIKINGS USE NORSE CODE?

THOSE WHO THINK they KNOW it all ARE ANNOYING TO THOSE OF US WHO DO!

EACHER LOVES me - SHE Puts kisses against All my sums

The only way to avoid mistakes is to gain experience
THe only way to gain experience ... is to make a mistake
IF WE LEARN FROM OUR MISTAKES I'm GETTING A FANTASTIC EDUCATION
NO PROBLEM IS SO BIG YOU CAN'T RUN AWAY FROM It
i can speak 8 languages
YES, BUT AL
AT THE SAM
TIME

don't do homework. no Teacher can blame you for something you haven't done

MY SISTER CAN PLAY THE PIANO BY EAR
I'D RATHER SHE WENT AND PLAYED IT OVER THERE!

I went home last night and my parents had moved house

youth is wasted on children

i MANAGED to miss the school bus again!

WHY IS WHISPERING NOT ALOUD?

AM I A BOY OR A GIRL?

NEITHER

I GOT –I IN MY EXAM. That's because I spelt my NAME WRONG AS WELL

I WON A PRIZE for PLAYING TRUANT

I DID'NT HAVE A PART IN THE SCHOOL PLAY

I GOT 'A' IN SPELLING

DOPE! THERE ISN'T AN 'A' IN SPELLING

ROO LOVES POOH

DAVID IS THE TYPE OF KID HIS MOTHER TOLD HIM NOT TO PLAY WITH

I'LL never learn to spell, teacher keeps changing the words
CROSSED-EYED TEACHERS CAN'T CONTROL THEIr PUPILS
BEETHOVEN WAS TONE DEAF.
PARDON? SIGNED LUDWIG
YOU HAVE TO KEEP A WATCH ON THE SWISS
GLUE

CAN WE HAVE OUR WALL BACK PLEASE?
90% OF HEADMASTERS TAKE 'THE GUARDIAN' The other 10% buy it
Monkey is the root to all people
ISAAC Newton was Right This is the centre of graffiti
I'm off my head Charles I
PAGE 19

GRAFFITI IN THE PLAYGROUND
GOD MADE ADAM BUT THOUGHT HE COULD DO BETTER SO HE MADE LITTLE GIRLS
DO RETIRING VOLKSWAGENS GO TO THE OLD VOLKS HOME?
MY sister USES MASSACRE ON HER EYES
EVERYONE WRITES ON WALLS BUT ME
FREE THE HEINZ 57
PAGE 20

IS AN ASPERSION A DONKEY FROM PERSIA ?

Is an asset a little donkey ?

CINDERELLA MARRIED FOR MONEY
SHE REALLY PUT HER FOOT IN IT !

WELLINGTON'S WIFE WAS AN OLD BOOT

THAT MAKES A PAIR OF 'EM

TIME FLIES AS THE MONKEY SAID when HE threw the clock AT The Cat

WOOD DOESN'T GROW ON TREES YOU KNOW
Save trees - eat a beaver
OWING TO A LACK OF INTEREST TOMORROW HAS BEEN CANCELLED
Nudists are people who wear one-button suits
ONLY DIRTY PEOPLE NEED TO WASH
PAGE 22

DO YOU HAVE TROUBLE MAKING UP YOUR MIND?
WELL, YES AND NO

An apple a day keeps the doctor away BUT AN ONION A DAY KEEPS EVERYONE AWAY

GRAFFITI DOESN'T GROW ON WALLS YOU KNOW

FOR the millionth time – stop exaggerating

I never used to be able to finish anything but now I

PRAKTISS
MAIKES
PURFIKT

IF YOU CANNOT COMMUNICATE
TRY TALKING

Nobody believes
I'm a liar
I don't believe you

WILL-IAM TELL WORE CONTACT LENSES

I think I'm a
Strawberry
YOU ARE IN A JAM
AREN'T YOU?

Old teachers never die they just grade away

My needlework teacher is a sew and sew!

MY WOODWORK TEACHER IS A CHIP OFF THE OLD BLOCK!

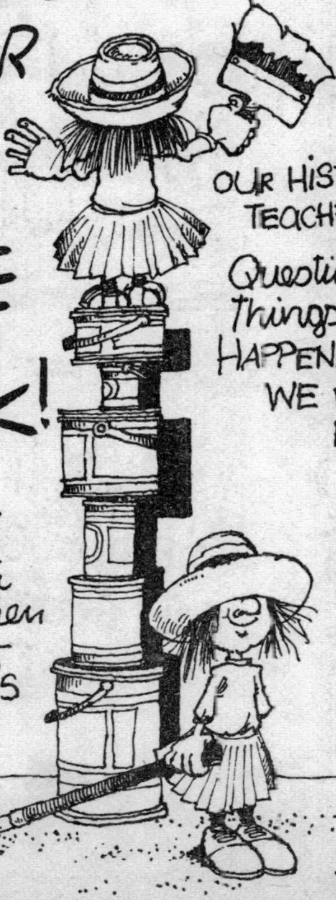

OUR HISTORY TEACHER KEEPS ASKING QUESTIONS ABOUT THINGS THAT HAPPENED BEFORE WE WERE EVEN BORN

I'm going to work in a bank when I grow up – I'm told there's money in it

MY TEACHER'S GOT A PRETTY FACE IF YOU CAN READ BETWEEN THE LINES
ISAAC NEWTON WAS A DOWN TO EARTH MAN
If it wasn't for Newton we'd all be eating bruised apples
Why are babies born so young?
MY BANK'S CALLED PIGGY

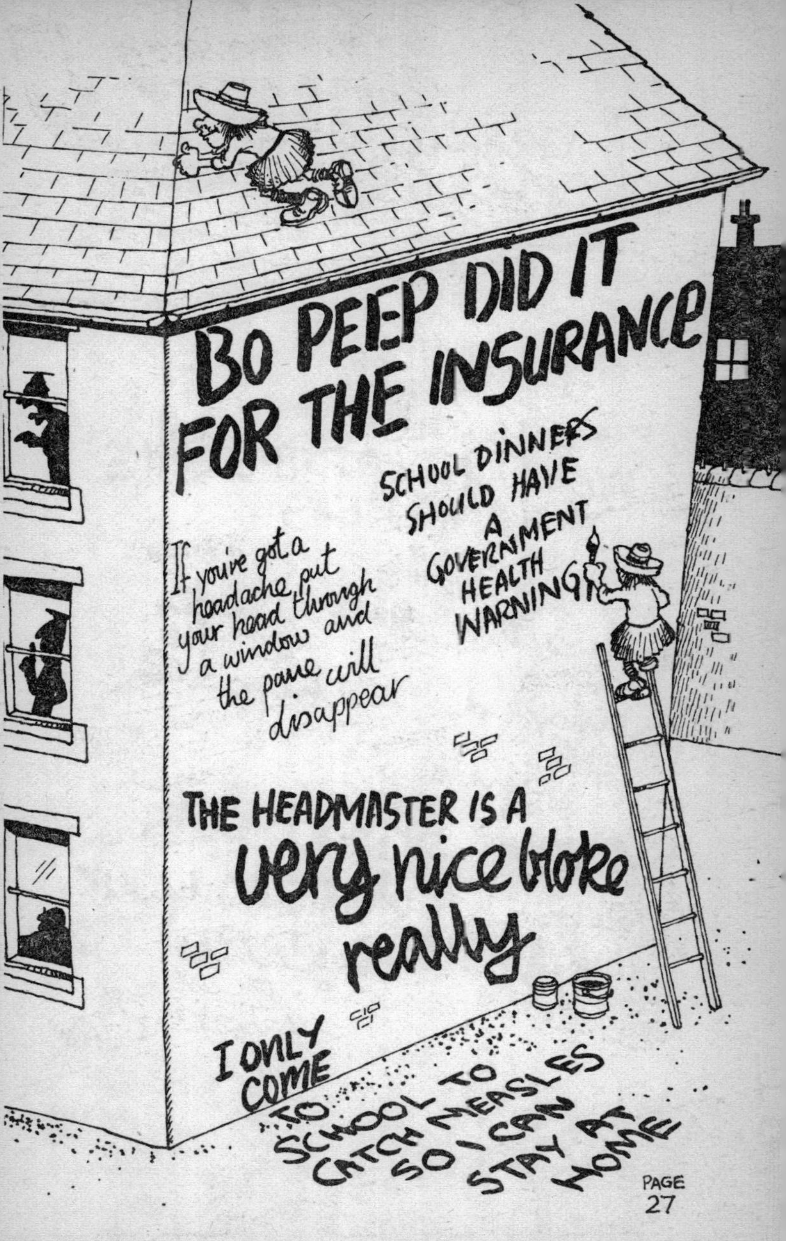
BO PEEP DID IT FOR THE INSURANCE
SCHOOL DINNERS SHOULD HAVE A GOVERNMENT HEALTH WARNING
If you've got a headache put your head through a window and the pane will disappear
THE HEADMASTER IS A very nice bloke really
I ONLY COME TO SCHOOL TO CATCH MEASLES SO I CAN STAY AT HOME

GRAFFITI IN THE SCHOOL CANTEEN

THE LUNCHPACK OF NOTRE DAME WAS HERE

I don't like my teacher

WELL JUST EAT THE CHIPS AND PEAS

Is this the face that shipped a thousand lunches?

SAUSAGE ROLLS, O.K.

Spinach puts colour in your cheeks

Who wants green cheeks?

O.K. SAUCE RULES, H.P.

The Graffiti here is tasteless

(signed) The Cook

Just like your food then

CAN I HAVE ANOTHER SLICE OF CUSTARD ?

KEEP THAT CAT OUT OF THE KITCHEN

otherwise it will be Cornish pasties for lunch tomorrow

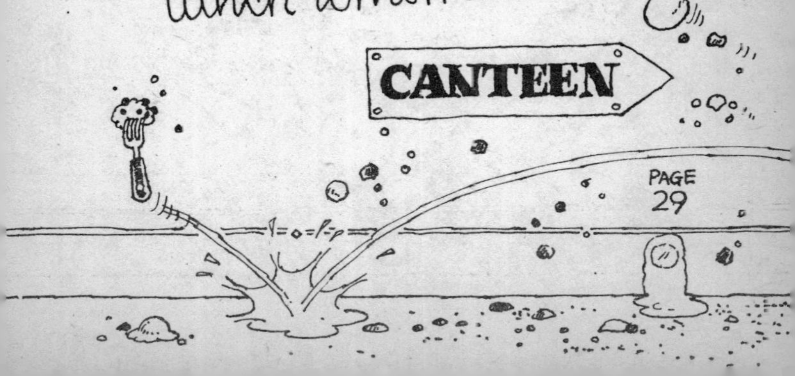

IS SHE HUNGARY?

ALASKA

YES SI AM

I'LL FIJI THEN

DON'T RUSSIA

My mother had a nervous breakdown trying to fit round tomatoes into square sandwiches
Everything comes to him who orders hash.
SWALLOW RAZOR BLADES? IT'LL SHARPEN YOUR APPETITE
fancy a bite? Dracula
THE FOOD HERE IS GOING TO WAIST

GRAFFITI AT THE SWIMMING BATHS

COMMUNICATE WITH A FISH— DROP IT A LINE

I DON'T LIKE SWIMMING IN MUDDY WATER

IT WASN'T MUDDY WHEN YOU GOT IN

Sing and shout and dance with joy
For I was here before Kilroy

Alas, my friend, before you spoke,
KILROY was here but his pencil broke.

would you call a swimming instructor a hold-up man?

TUTANKHAMUN HAS CHANGED HIS MIND AND WANTS TO BE BURIED AT SEA

BEWARE THE MAN-Eating SHARK

BEWARE THE BOY EATING SARDINES

Between your eyes is something that smells

THE OPTICIAN'S DAUGHTER KEEPS MAKING A SPECTACLE OF HERSELF

PAIN PROVES YOU'RE ALIVE

Tooth-hurty is the only time to go to the dentist

modesty is wearing swimming trunks with sleeves

why is water wet?

The Water in this pool is freezing—
THAT'S COOL, MAN!

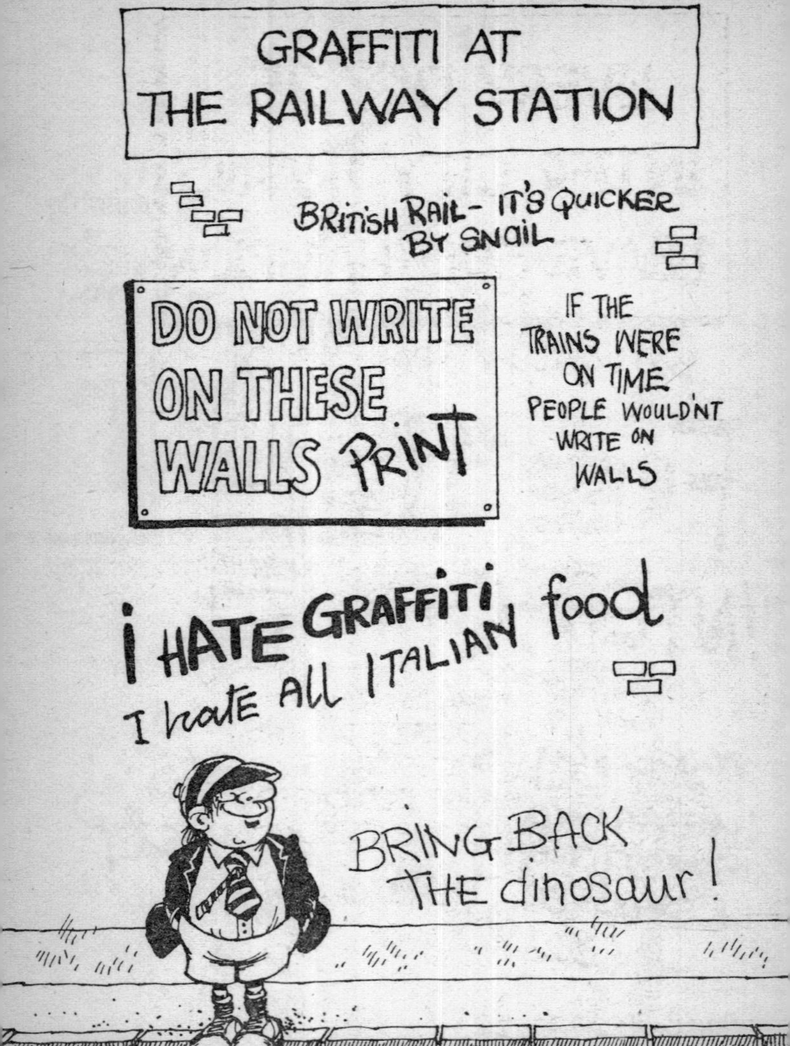
GRAFFITI AT THE RAILWAY STATION
BRITISH RAIL - IT'S QUICKER BY SNAIL
DO NOT WRITE ON THESE WALLS PRINT
IF THE TRAINS WERE ON TIME PEOPLE WOULDN'T WRITE ON WALLS
i HATE GRAFFITI
I hate ALL ITALIAN food
BRING BACK THE dinosaur!

EVERY DAY 25
INTER-CITY TRAINS
LEAVE SOUTHAMPTON
but only 7 get back
FREE THE
INTER-CITY 125
BRITISH RAIL
ADVISE THAT THIS
FOOTPATH IS
NOT DEDICATED
TO THE PUBLIC
neither is British
Rail

TOWER HILL RETURN PLEASE
AND A SINGLE FOR THE WIFE
HOW DO YOU WAKE UP THE SLEEPING CAR?
BEETHOVEN WAS SO DEAF HE THOUGHT HE WAS A PAINTER
The Graffiti on British Rail is like the food on British Rail - Terrible
PAINT
PAGE 38

The Great train Robbery happens every DAY WHEN YOU BUY A CUP OF BRITISH RAIL Coffee

WARNING
PASSENGERS ARE REQUESTED NOT TO CROSS THE LINES

It takes hours to untangle them

GOD Made Things that CREEP And CRAWL But BRITISH RAIL IT BEATS THEM ALL

STOP, LOOK, AND LISTEN AND be HIT BY A TRAIN

why aren't trains on time? be thankful they're on the track BRITISH RAIL

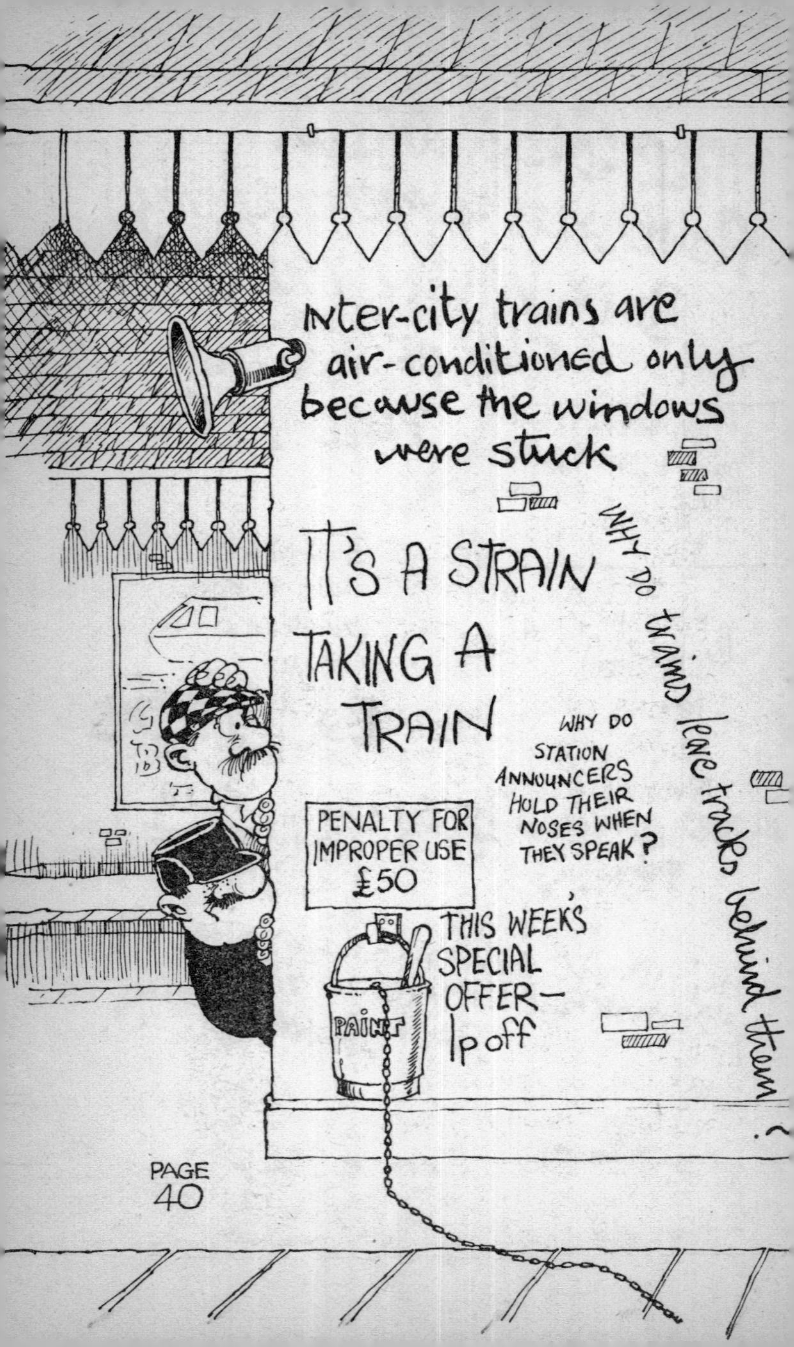

inter-city trains are air-conditioned only because the windows were stuck
IT'S A STRAIN TAKING A TRAIN
WHY DO trains leave tracks behind them?
WHY DO STATION ANNOUNCERS HOLD THEIR NOSES WHEN THEY SPEAK?
PENALTY FOR IMPROPER USE £50
THIS WEEK'S SPECIAL OFFER– 1p off
PAINT

I wanted a sandwich but dad had forgotten his cheque book

BRITISH RAIL ARE AMAZING– IF THE TRAIN'S ON TIME IT'S AMAZING

I only wanted a ticket to Enfield, I didn't ask to buy the station

NEVER RACE TRAINS TO CROSSINGS. IF IT'S A TIE, YOU LOSE.

I'd travel by train more often but I'm so afraid of meeting Jimmy Savile

GRAFFITI AT THE CINEMA

Mickey Mouse is A Rat

FRANKENSTEIN WAS LONELY UNTIL HE LEARNT HOW TO MAKE NEW FRIENDS

Noddy has big ears

JAWS
3
JUST WHEN
YOU THOUGHT
IT WAS SAFE
TO HAVE A BATH

Watership Down
You've read the book
You've seen the film
Now try the stew

LEGALISE
TELEPATHY

I knew you
were going to
say that

JULIUS
CAESAR
BY
WILLIAM
SHAKESPEARE

A shortened version
of Julius-grab-
the-girl-quickly-before-
she-gets-away

I'm a vampire - please wash your neck

DRACULA IS A PAIN IN THE NECK

There's a horror at the cinema - I daren't buy an ice-cream from her during the interval

I used to be a Werewolf but I'm all right Nowoooooooooooooh!

THE STRONGEST MAN IN THE WORLD

ALL WEAK

IS A PAS DE DEUX A FATHER OF TWINS?

Only if Coq au Vin is a chicken on a lorry

tarzan is a swinger

DRACULA LOVES IN VEIN

Put Cement in your lemonade and have a stiff drink

HAVE YOU SEEN THE INVISIBLE MAN LATELY?

This wall is available in paperback
WHO WAS CORPORAL PUNISHMENT?
I'VE SEEN THE FILM THREE TIMES
James Bond rules, OOK
C-3PO IS GOING RUSTY
THE HORROR FROM PLANET EARTH
Miss Peabody from the Chemistry lab.
PAGE 46

The pen is mightier than the pencil

PAINT IS MIGHTIER THAN THE PEN

GET THE MONSTER BEFORE IT GETS ----- UGH ----

My favourite film is about cricket - its called 'The Umpire strikes back'

CAN YOU HELP ME OUT?
Which way did you come in?

If superman is so clever why does he wear his underpants over his clothes?

HE WHO LAUGHS LAST DOESN'T GET THE JOKE

GRAFFITI AT THE AIRPORT

TERMINAL
ENTRANCE
PAGE
49

BREAKFAST IN LONDON!
LUNCH IN NEW YORK
Luggage in Bermuda

Travel broadens the mind
Is that why you've got a fat head?

I HATE BEING in the air in A PLANE
I'd hate to be in the air without one

THIS WALL IS APPROVED TO BRITISH STANDARD NO. 29078
So was the Titanic

lightning can't conduct itself

IS A JUMBO JET AN ELEPHANT THAT FLIES?
That's Dumbo you idiot

I just flew in from Sydney
I BET YOUR ARMS ARE TIRED!
I bet Sydney's relieved

air travel is A way of seeing less and less of more and more

Visit a beautiful spot in the world where the hand of man has never set foot

SOON YOU'LL BE ABLE TO FLY AROUND THE WORLD IN JUST FOUR HOURS

One hour to fly and three to get to the airport

IF GOD HAD MEANT US TO FLY HE WOULD HAVE GIVEN US WINGS OR SENT US THE TICKETS

Dogs and small children must be carried on the escalator

If you don't have a dog a cat will do

I FEEL SICK JUST LICKING AN AIRMAIL STAMP

I'VE LIVED ON EARTH ALL MY LIFE

i'd rather eat food personally

PARIS IS WONDERFUL. IF YOU EVER GO THERE DON'T MISS IT.

ESCALATORS ARE ON THE WAY UP

EXITS ARE ON THE WAY OUT

BAD SPELLERS OF THE WORLD UNTIE

GRAFFITI ON THE SPORTS FIELD

Miss Piggy for Games teacher!

I WATCH UNITED PLAY FOOTBALL EVERY SATURDAY

Do they ever come and see you when you're sick?

WEST HAM FOR THE CUP!

Chelsea for the Saucer

A Broken leg's not what it's cracked up to be

Bolton are magic. Watch them disappear from the second division

I DON'T CARE IF I WIN OR LOSE, AS LONG AS I WIN

I THINK, THEREFORE I AM,
I AM, THEREFORE I THINK.
I'M PINK. THEREFORE I'M SPAM

IT SAYS TEAR ALONG the dotted line - couldn't I just walk?

when you get old do the calves of your legs become cows?

APATHY RULES

SO WHAT?

JUST WHEN I WAS GETTING USED TO YESTERDAY ALONG CAME TODAY

Every dog has its day, but only a dog with a broken tail has a weak end

I won a cup for boxing

IT WAS TO PUT YOUR teeth in

Is clumsiness catching

NO, droppin

EVERYONE WRITES ON WALLS BUT ME

GO AND BITE A FISHERMAN. HE MIGHT NOT HAVE HAD A BITE ALL DAY
I shot a hole in one
Poor JUAN!
WOULD SPECTATORS PLEASE BE QUIET DURING MATCHES
AND LET THE PLAYERS RAISE A RACKET
TELEPATHY IS A CODE INVENTED BY MORSE
I SCORED TEN GOALS TODAY
PITY THEY WERE IN YOUR OWN GOAL
PAGE 55

GRAFFITI AT THE BUS STATION
FOUND: ONE PAIR OF GLASSES
PLEASE WRITE LARGER, I'VE LOST MY GLASSES
'LONG WALK' BY MISS. D. BUS
WALLS HAVE EARS
Yeh, I just found one in my ice-cream
KEEP THIS BUS TIDY
throw your tickets out of the window

IS THERE INTELLIGENT LIFE ON EARTH ?
Yes, but I'm only visiting
The only way to get a seat on a bus is to become a bus driver
PLEASE HAVE THE EXACT FARE READY
and Shock THE conductor
MIND THAT CHILD
Aim for teacher

BUSES STOP HERE
if you're lucky
KINDLY PASS ALONG THE BUS AND SO MAKE ROOM FOR ALL OF US
THAT'S ALL RIGHT WITHOUT A DOUBT BUT ONCE INSIDE YOU CAN'T GET OUT
we have ways of making you walk
NOTHING GOES FASTER THAN A BUS YOU JUST MISSED
I TAKE THE BUS HOME EVERY DAY BUT MOTHER MAKES ME BRING IT BACK

IF YOU CAN'T READ, WATCH THIS SPACE
Pedestrians must walk
WHY DO BUSES GOING IN THE OPPOSITE DIRECTION ALWAYS HAVE EMPTY SEATS?
IF YOU MISS A BUS DON'T PANIC - COUNT TO TEN - Then panic

GRAFFITI IN THE STREET
I've been cured of indecision. AT least I think I have
BEWARE OF SCHOOL CHILDREN
ESPECIALLY IF DRIVING CARS
SNOOPY HAS FLEAS

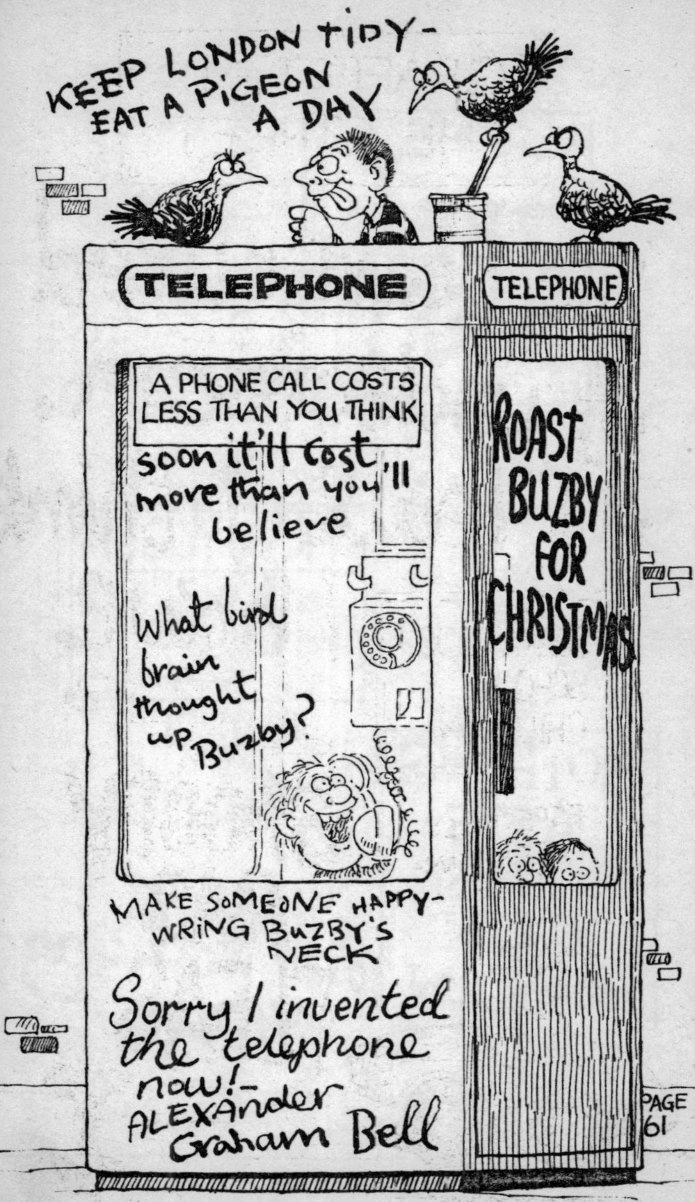
KEEP LONDON TIDY-
EAT A PIGEON
A DAY
TELEPHONE
TELEPHONE
A PHONE CALL COSTS
LESS THAN YOU THINK
soon it'll cost more than you'll believe
What bird brain thought up Buzby?
ROAST BUZBY FOR CHRISTMAS
MAKE SOMEONE HAPPY-
WRING BUZBY'S
NECK
Sorry I invented the telephone now! - ALEXander Graham Bell
PAGE
61

POLICE NOTICE

BE ALERT

Your country needs lerts

Be aloof Your country's got enough lerts

TRY YOGA

It's made with real fruit

NOTHING ACTS FASTER THAN ANADIN

Take nothing then

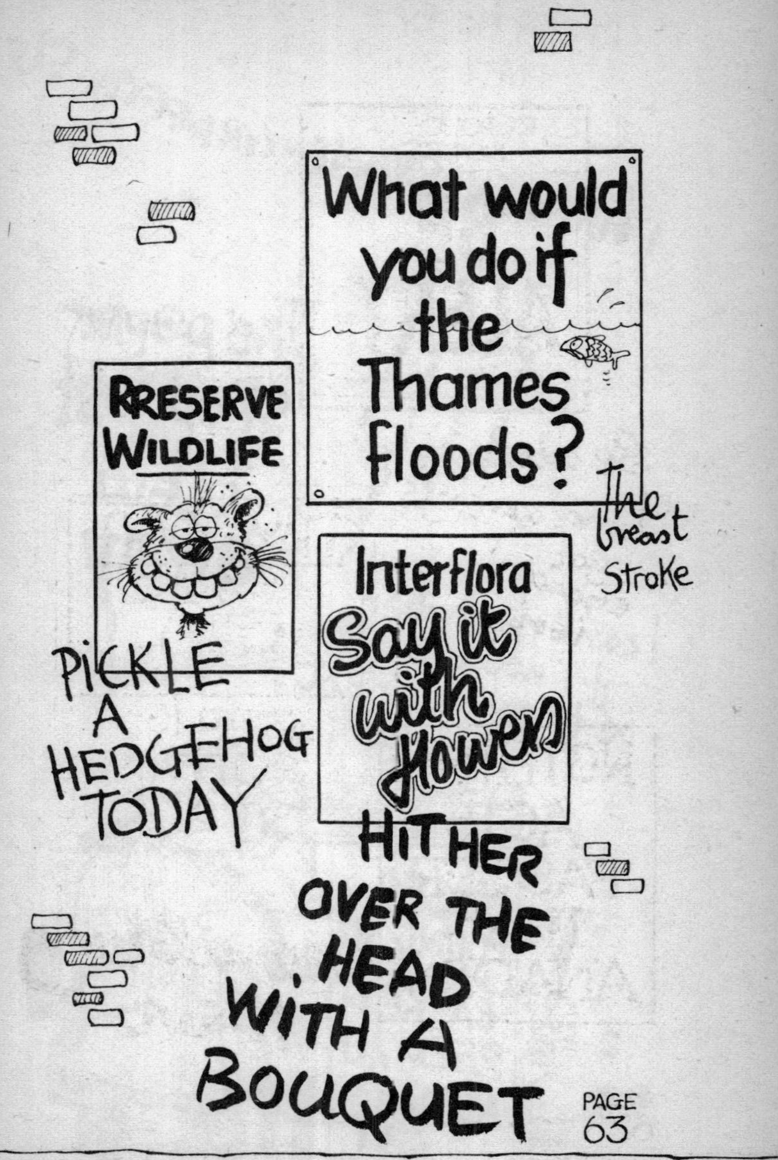

What would you do if the Thames floods?
The breast stroke
RRESERVE WILDLIFE
PICKLE A HEDGEHOG TODAY
Interflora
Say it with flowers
HIT HER OVER THE HEAD WITH A BOUQUET
PAGE 63

EVERYBODY HATES GRAFFITIISTS
I HATE EVERYONE - GRAFFITIISTS
Keep smiling - everyone will wonder what you've been up to
The paper shop just blew away
I can't remember if I used to be forgetful or not
MOSES FOUND IN A BASKET- REED ALL ABOUT IT
PAGE 64

KEEP BRITAIN TIDY

Post your rubbish abroad

Vick gets right up my nose

well tell him to come down then

THE ANNUAL CONFERENCE OF FORTUNE-TELLERS HAS BEEN CANCELLED DUE TO UNFORESEEN CIRCUMSTANCES

Living on earth is expensive but it does include an annual free trip round the sun

Do unto others before they get a chance to do it unto you

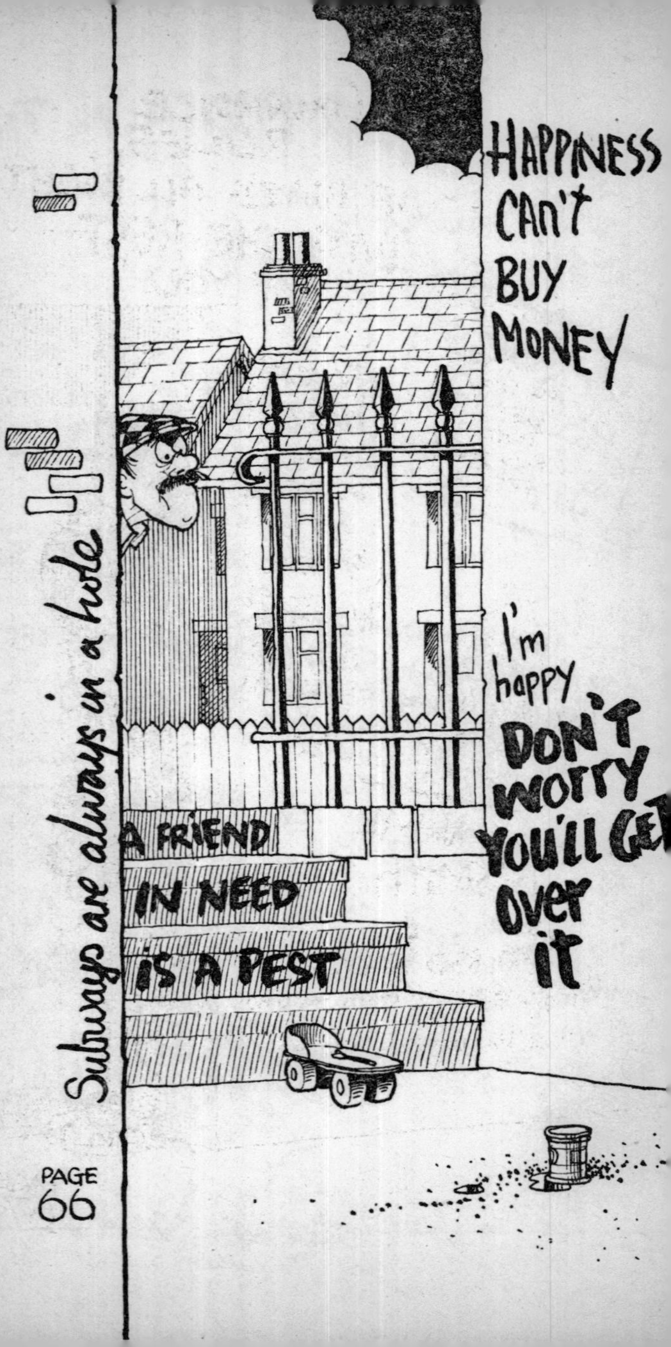
Subways are always in a hole
HAPPINESS CAN'T BUY MONEY
I'm happy
DON'T WORRY YOU'LL GET OVER IT
A FRIEND IN NEED IS A PEST

COWARDICE RULES,.. IF THAT'S ALL RIGHT WITH THE REST OF YOU
DON'T PLAY IN THE STREET - YOU MAY GET THAT RUN DOWN FEELING
never hit a man when he's down
He might get up again.
Does this belong to you? The name is smudged
No, MY NAME IS SMITH
I'm no fool
What's your opinion against a thousand others?

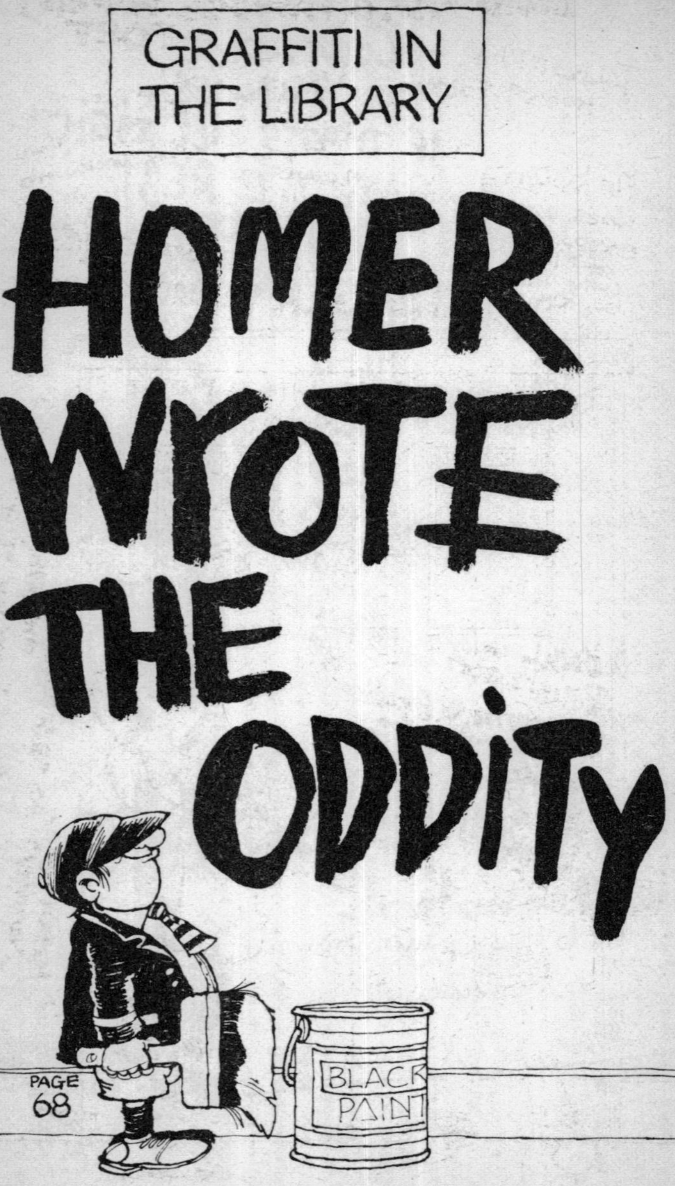
GRAFFITI IN THE LIBRARY
HOMER WROTE THE ODDITY
PAGE 68
BLACK PAINT

LIVID WAS A FAMOUS ROMAN POET
TOLKEIN IS HOBBIT FORMING
Yorick is a numb skull
Alas poor Kilroy, I knew him backwards
Mr kipling does write exceedingly good books
Biggles flies back to front
LIBRARY
THE FRENCH NATIONAL ANTHEM IS THE MAYONNAISE
T.S. Eliot is an anagram of toilets
THE LIBRARIAN DISAPPROVES OF LAVATORY JOKES
Basil Brush for headmaster!
PAGE 69

If you're a librarian can you whistle while you work?
the Venus de Milo is perfectly armless
If you cannot read watch this space for further details.
I may BE iLLITERATE BUT AT LEAST I CAN READ
VAN GOGH WAS EAR
PAGE 70

If you cannot spell a word correctly look in a Dikshunary
IF ALL THE WORLD'S A STAGE AND MEN AND WOMEN MERELY PLAYERS, WHERE DOES THE AUDIENCE COME FROM?
BE QUIET WHEN YOU TALK TO ME
The librarian tells me I'm a good book-keeper

the only good Books are read ones
the Pope lives in the Vacuum
FICTION is A FACT
WORDS MEAN NOTHING TODAY
PAGE 72

LAUGH AND THE WORLD LAUGHS WITH YOU

BUT YOU'LL BE TOLD TO LEAVE THE LIBRARY

Jacob had a brother called see-saw

Poetry is when every line starts with a capital letter

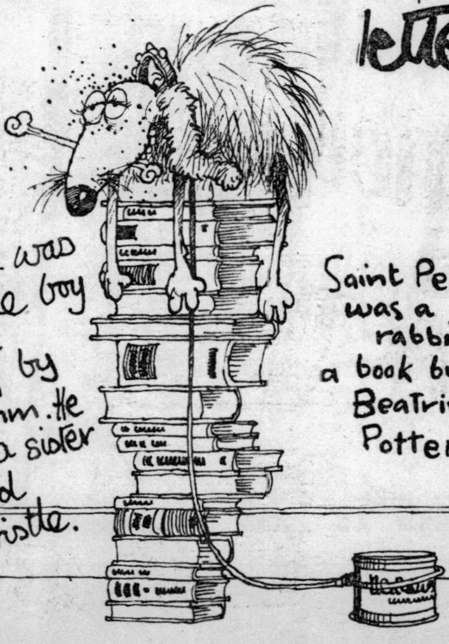

Handel was a little boy in a story by Grimm. He had a sister called Gristle.

Saint Peter was a rabbit in a book by Beatrix Potter

JOHN LOGIE BAIRD
BY TILLY VISION
DOGS DINNER
BY NORA BONE
THE SUBURBS
BY BILL TUPPAREA
THE BANK RAID
BY HANS UPP
TUG OF WAR
BY PAUL HARD
HAIR CARE
BY DAN DRUFF
PAPER FLOWERS
BY R. T. FISCHALL
PAGE 74

OVER THE CLIFF BY HUGO FIRST
THE HOUSING PROBLEM
BY RUFUS QUICK
IS IT POSSIBLE? BY IZZY ABLE AND WILLIE DOOIT
The Army
BY MILLY TERRY AND REGGIE MENTALL
METRICATION BY MILLIE METRE
SLEEP BY ANNIE STETHIC
In the Country BY THERESA GREEN

EVERY MAN REAPS WHAT HE SOWS

EXCEPT THE AMATEUR GARDENER

THE WORLD WILL END ON FRIDAY

I hadn't any plans for the week-end anyway

Laugh and the world thinks you're an idiot

IS A DOGGEREL A LITTLE DOG?

Geography is spreading all over the world

STOP GEOGRAPHY NOW!

SOVIET IS ANOTHER NAME FOR A TABLE NAPKIN

SHAKESPEARE WROTE TRAGEDY, COMEDY AND ERRORS

SEE A PIN AND PICK IT UP AND ALL DAY LONG YOU'LL HAVE A PIN

Gorgons had snakes in their hair and looked like women only more horrible

GRAFFITI IN THE FARMYARD
WHY DO COWS HAVE BELLS?
Don't be silly, they have horns
BUT THE HORNS DON'T WORK
That's why they have bells, you fool
The cow jumped over the moon because the farmer had cold hands
Do chickens get people pox?
PAGE 78

THERE'S SOMETHING ABOUT A FARM THAT GETS YOU
ESPECIALLY IF THE WIND'S IN THE WRONG DIRECTION
FREE ACCESS TO THE FIELD
The Bull changes
Flowers rule, bouquet
WHY DID THE CHICKEN CROSS THE ROAD? BECAUSE IT SAW THE ZEBRA CROSSING
Which proves that chickens are copy cats
Help Australian oaks
Plant an acorn upside down
CATTLE PLEASE CLOSE THE GATE
CLEVER COWS ROUND HERE

GRAFFITI AT THE ZOO

IF YOU CROSS AN ELEPHANT WITH A GOLDFISH WOULD YOU GET SWIMMING TRUNKS?

NEVER PLAY GAMES HERE – THERE ARE TOO MANY CHEETAHS

CROSS AN ALLIGATOR WITH A PARROT AND YOU'LL GET A BIRD THAT SHOUTS 'WHO'S A PRETTY BOY?' AS IT BITES YOUR ARM OFF!

NEXT TIME YOU HAVE A SORE THROAT BE THANKFUL YOU'RE NOT A GIRAFFE

DO NOT WALK ON THE GRASS

Jump on it

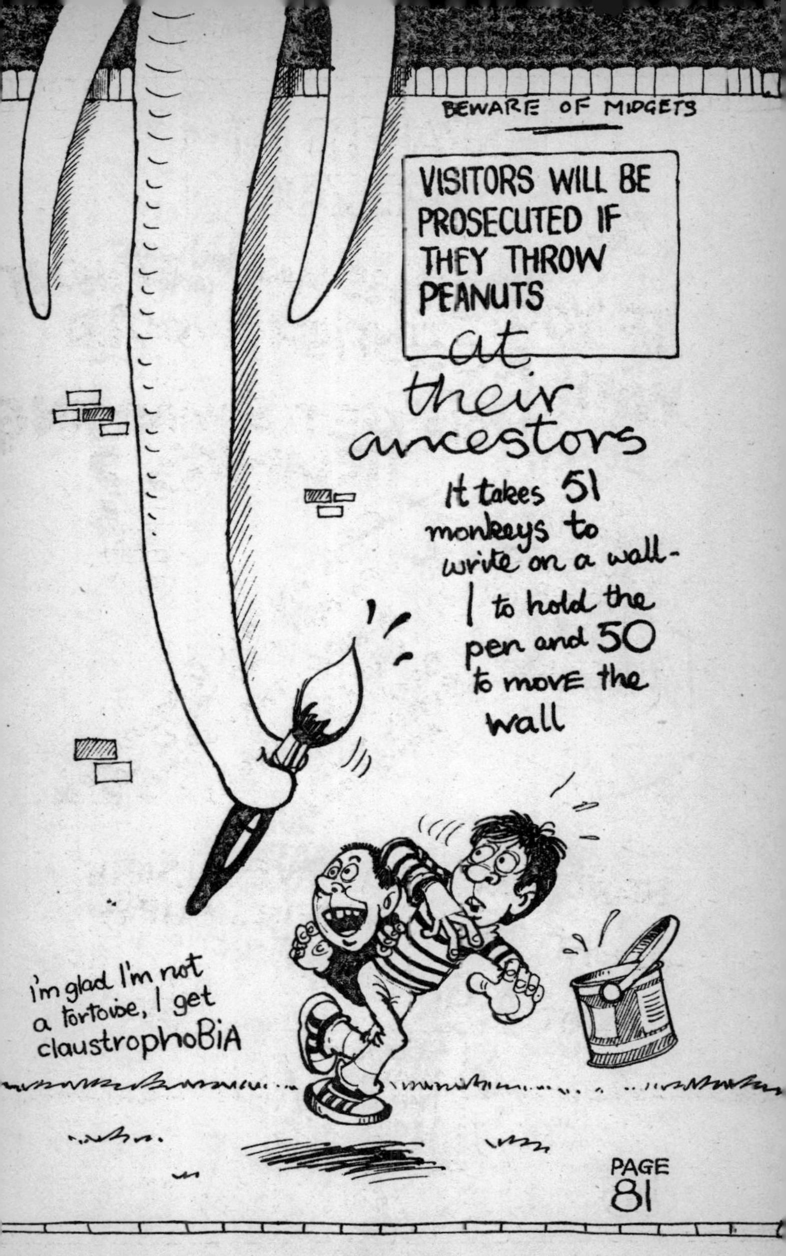

BEWARE OF MIDGETS
VISITORS WILL BE PROSECUTED IF THEY THROW PEANUTS at their ancestors
It takes 51 monkeys to write on a wall - 1 to hold the pen and 50 to move the wall
i'm glad I'm not a tortoise, I get claustrophoBiA

The best way to talk to a lion is by Long-distance telephone
SORRY, LION'S BUSY
I CAME TO THE ZOO WHEN I WAS SEVEN
Which cage were you in?
AN ELEPHANT NEVER FORGETS, BUT WHAT HAS HE GOT TO REMEMBER?
Have you been to the zoo before?
As a visitor I mean
WET PAINT
This is not an instruction

Once there was an elephant who went away to forget

ELEPHANTS ARE MODEST – THEY ALWAYS BATHE WITH THEIR TRUNKS

I can lift an elephant with one hand

WHERE DO YOU FIND A ONE-HANDED ELEPHANT THOUGH?

You can always tell an elephant by the smell of peanuts on its breath

MY BROTHER NEEDS TWO TICKETS, ONE TO GET IN, AND ONE TO GET OUT

GRAFFITI AT THE SHOPS

HOW MANY WINDOWS DID YOU BUY?

I CAN ONLY AFFORD TO GO WINDOW SHOPPING

The cost of living is killing

I'm saving money
ONE DAY IT'LL BE WORTH SOMETHING
Never!

YOU CAN'T TAKE YOUR MONEY WITH YOU WHEN YOU DIE
I can't afford not to!

Why does mum say she's been shopping when she hasn't bought anything?

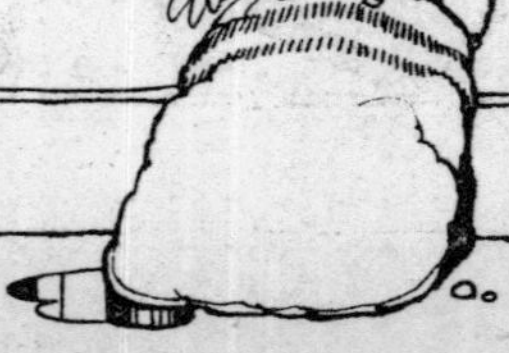

SHORT-SIGHTED PEOPLE RULE, OK

Visit the
CORNER Market
Buy two corners
TODAY'S
PIGS ARE
TOMORROW'
BACON
WANTED
Someone to iron, wash and milk two cows
WOMAN WANTED TO RUN UP CURTAINS
Bird for sale.
GOING CHEEP
BURGLARS RULE OK

Why does Christmas lways come when the shops are so busy?
VISIT THE BARGAIN BASEMENT
UPSTAIRS
ShopLifters have the gift of thE Grab
OPEN
PAGE 87

GRAFFITI AT THE DISCO

MODERN MUSIC ISN'T AS BAD AS IT SOUNDS

Nostalgia rules, Hokey cokey!

I don't think I know the steps to that one, How do you do it?

What did we do before nostalgia?

dancers run in my family

Pity they don't dance

Sheena is a good Dancer

That's not dancing, someone spilt coffee in her lap

HOW IS THE WINTER OF OUR DISCOTHEQUE?

I GET ON WITH EVERONE

Except people and animals

NOSTALGIA'S A THING OF THE PAST

TO MORROW IS JUST A NOTHER DAY
I'VE SEEN A BARN DANCE
Well, I've seen a moth ball
If you can read this you're dancing upside down
I learnt to dance in one evening
I THOUGHT SO
Drums take A LOT OF BEATING

'F you get a bad back here its called a slipped disco
Are discos dark so that you can't see whose toes you're treading on?
I CAN'T SEE BECAUSE IT'S DARK, I'M DEAFENED BY THE MUSIC, AND PEOPLE KEEP TRAMPLING ALL OVER ME - WHY DO WE CALL IT FUN?
I could dance like this forever
Don't you EVER want to improve?
If you know the steps you're obviously doing the wrong dance

GRAFFITI IN THE DOCTOR'S SURGERY

I'VE GOT A BAD STOMACH

keep your coat done up and nobody will notice

Is there an imaginary cure for hypochondria?

WHAT CAN I TAKE FOR KLEPTOMANIA?

I SCRATCHED MY HEAD AND FOUND A SPLINTER IN MY FINGER

my doctor keeps losing his patients

CONSULT A DOCTOR
you'll never live to regret it

Don't lose any sleep over insomnia

I'm suffering from
a
pain
in
my leg
What else can you do with it?

BEWARE OF THE DOC

CAN I TAKE MY MEDICINE WITH A FORK ?

The doctors been taken ill

I want a cure for my cold that will keep me off school for two months

Stop a head cold going to your chest — tie a knot in your neck

I think I'm Allergic to school

HYPOCHONDRIA KILLS, OK?

Eventually

Doctors are making great progress — what used to be an itch is now an Allergy

DYSLEXIA RULES, K.O.

Operations are funny because they leave you in stitches

I've got such bad handwriting teacher says I should be a doctor....

I'm so unlucky
I even get
caught writing
graf
ENOUGH IS
ENOUGH. O.K.!